W9-AMO-275

GREGORY L. VOGT

ASTEROIDS, COMETS, AND METEORS

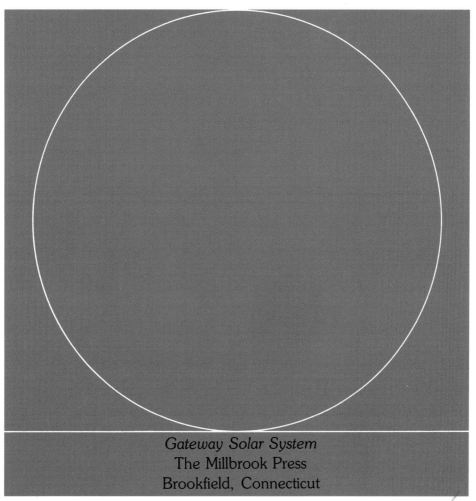

Gateway Solar System
The Millbrook Press
Brookfield, Connecticut

Library of Congress Cataloging-in-Publication Data
Vogt, Gregory.
Asteroids, comets, and meteors / Gregory L. Vogt.
p.   cm.
Includes bibliographical references and index.
Summary: Presents information on the different types of celestial
matter known as asteroids, comets, and meteors and on what
scientists learned from the impact of a comet on the surface of
Jupiter.
ISBN 1-56294-601-3 (Lib. bdg.)
1. Comets—Juvenile literature.   2. Asteroids—Juvenile
literature.   3. Meteors—Juvenile literature.   [1. Comets.
2. Asteroids.   3. Meteors.]   I. Title.
QB721.5.V64   1996
523.6—dc20   95-19735   CIP   AC

Published by the Millbrook Press, Inc.
2 Old New Milford Road
Brookfield, Connecticut 06804

ASTEROIDS, COMETS, AND METEORS

Comets are made of ice, dust, gas, and rock, and have long, ghostly tails that stream away from the Sun. This picture of Halley's comet was taken by the European Space Agency's *Giotto* space-craft as the comet passed near the Sun in 1986.

Discovery

Everyone is good at something. Carolyn Shoemaker is an *astronomer,* a scientist who studies objects in outer space. Discovering comets is what she does better than just about anyone else.

Comets are some of the most beautiful and mysterious objects in our solar system. Made of rock, dust, ice, and frozen gas, comets mostly travel in long, looping *orbits* far away from the Sun. When they do get near the Sun, the Sun's heat thaws some of the ice and gas. White ribbons of thawed gas stream away from the comet to form a ghostly tail that is sometimes millions of miles long and visible from Earth.

On the night of March 25, 1993, Carolyn Shoemaker, her geologist husband Eugene, and amateur astronomer David Levy were searching for comets. The team was using the 18-inch (0.46-meter) Schmidt telescope at the Palomar Observatory in southern California as a camera to take pictures. First, they would take one picture and then, 40 minutes later, they would take a second picture of the same place in the sky.

Carolyn would search the pictures for comets. To do so, she used a device that could examine both pictures at the same time. Through this device, stars and other very distant objects look flat, but comets, because they are fast moving, look as if they are floating above or below the background, depending upon the direction they are traveling in. The changing position of the comet in the two pictures gives the illusion of three dimensions. The effect is similar to colorful "magic pictures" that you have to look at in just the right way to see the hidden objects.

The weather that night wasn't very clear. David even suggested that he and Eugene use some film that had been damaged and save the good film for a better night. They took their pictures and gave them to Carolyn to examine. Carolyn studied the pictures carefully and discovered something new. She found a long smudge floating above the background. "I think I've found a squashed comet!" she announced.

The squashed comet that Carolyn Shoemaker thought she found turned out not to be a single comet,

Carolyn Shoemaker's "squashed" comet was, in fact, 21 fragments of a comet that had disintegrated near Jupiter, as shown in this highly magnified NASA photo.

but fragments from a larger comet that had broken apart. When astronomers later looked at pictures taken by NASA's Hubble Space Telescope, they found that the squashed comet was really 21 separate large fragments. Each fragment was following the same orbit as the parent comet. In the NASA pictures, the beautiful train of fragments resembled a string of pearls. As is the custom when comets are discovered, this comet was named P/Shoemaker-Levy 9, after its discoverers.

Leftovers

Billions of years ago, our *solar system* formed in space from a great cloud of gas, dust, and debris. Most of the material fell into the center of the cloud to form the Sun. Just about all that was left condensed to form 9 planets and more than 60 moons. The little that remained clumped together to form a much smaller class of objects, which we call comets, asteroids, and meteors. Today, these objects orbit the Sun at widely varying distances and at times come very close to Earth.

Asteroids

Asteroids are large chunks of rock and metal that orbit the Sun. They range from just over 1/2 mile (1 kilometer) to a few hundred miles in *diameter*. The largest known asteroid is Ceres, which is nearly 600 miles (950 kilometers) in diameter.

Most asteroids travel in the wide gap between the planets Mars and Jupiter. This region is called the *asteroid belt*. A few asteroids travel in paths across Mars's orbit, and some even cross Earth's orbit. The exact number of asteroids is unknown, but astronomers estimate there may be 100,000. About 4.5 billion years ago, however, there were trillions of asteroids circling the infant Sun. Most of these chunks came together to form the planets and their moons. The asteroids that astronomers can count today are just the few leftovers from the early solar system.

Asteroids are so small and so far away that it is difficult to see them, even through powerful telescopes. So astronomers group them into different categories based on the way they reflect sunlight.

The asteroid belt is divided into an inner belt and an outer belt. The *inner belt,* asteroids that are within 250 million miles (400 million kilometers) of the Sun, appears to contain asteroids that are made primarily of metals. These asteroids are so rich in metals that some scientists have suggested that a space mission be sent out to capture one and bring it back to Earth's orbit. Future space miners could mine the metals for use on Earth.

The *outer belt,* asteroids 250 million miles (400 million kilometers) beyond the Sun, consists of rocky asteroids. These asteroids are darker than the asteroids of the inner belt. They are rich in carbon and in minerals that contain water.

In 1991 an asteroid was studied close up for the first time. On its way to Jupiter, the *Galileo* spacecraft, launched by the National Aeronautics and Space Administration (NASA), flew near the asteroid Gaspra. The pictures from *Galileo* showed that Gaspra, because of its shape and the many craters on its surface, looks like a potato. Gaspra, and probably all the other asteroids, had been marred by many collisions with other objects in space.

Nearly two years later, *Galileo* passed the asteroid Ida. Astronomers who studied Ida's picture were not

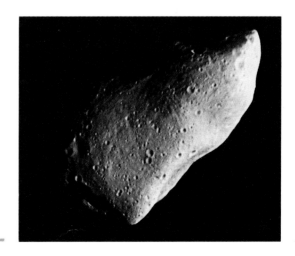

The surface of the asteroid Gaspra, a 12 by 7½ mile (19 by 12 kilometer) chunk of space rock, has more than 600 craters.

When scientists studied this photograph of asteroid Ida, they were surprised to find a small object to the right of it. This was their first proof that asteroids could have satellites. Ida, cratered by collisions with other objects in space, is almost 40 times larger than its satellite, which is 1 mile (1.5 kilometers) in diameter.

surprised that it too looked like a potato. But they were surprised by something else: On the picture there was a small dot near Ida. The dot turned out to be a small space rock orbiting Ida, just as the Moon orbits Earth!

Comets

One of the most beautiful sights in our solar system occurs when a comet travels near the Sun. One night, the sky appears ordinary, and the next, a fuzzy star with a ghostly white tail appears. Over the next several weeks, the tail gets brighter and longer, sometimes stretching for more than 60 million miles (100 million kilometers) across space. After the comet passes the Sun, its tail shrinks and grows dimmer, and then the comet is gone.

Comets are actually dirty ice balls, usually measuring from about 0.6 to 6.2 miles (1 to 10 kilometers) in diameter. Many comets travel around the Sun in long, looping orbits that bring them near the Sun at one end and well beyond Jupiter at the other end.

The orbit of each comet is different. Some, like Halley's comet, named after the astronomer Edmund Halley, take only about 75 years to orbit the Sun. Other comets travel in orbits so large that they take tens of thousands of years to complete.

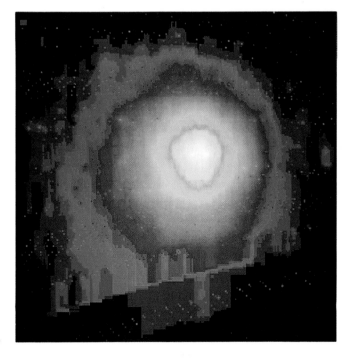

Halley's comet orbits the Sun approximately every 75 years. When it came close to Earth in 1986, a fleet of spacecraft was waiting to study it. Color has been added to this picture taken by NASA's *Pioneer Venus* spacecraft to show changes in the brightness of the comet's atmosphere.

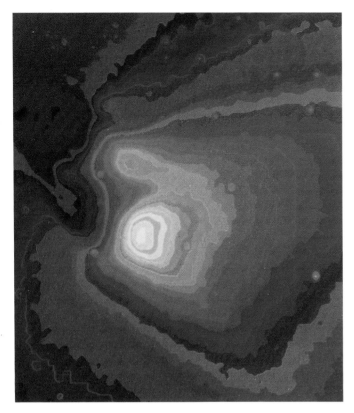

The nucleus of the comet is the dark spot in the upper left corner of this photograph. The brightest area is a jet of dust and gas erupting from the nucleus and glowing in the sunlight. This photo of Halley's comet was taken by the European Space Agency's spacecraft *Giotto* from 12,430 miles (20,000 kilometers) away.

The icy, hard part of a comet is called the *nucleus.* When a comet nears the Sun, the heat begins melting some of the ice and frozen chemicals locked inside the nucleus. Gas and dust are released and form an atmosphere, or *coma,* around the nucleus. Coma is the Greek word for hair. Because of its coma, a comet looks like a star with long hair. Comets were sometimes referred to as bearded stars. The coma can grow into a vast gas and dust cloud, bigger than the planet Jupiter.

Some of the gas and dust coming off a comet is blown by the *solar wind*—the particle streams that move outward from the Sun. The solar wind blows the gas and dust away from the coma to form a long tail. No matter which way the comet is traveling, the tail always points away from the Sun.

Each time a comet passes near the Sun, about 3 feet (1 meter) of its surface melts away. After the comet has made several hundred or thousand trips near the Sun, all that is left of it is a rocky core that resembles an asteroid. If comets, like every other object in our solar system, were created billions of years ago, astronomers wonder why we still see them. Their ice and dust should have melted and blown away long ago. The solution to this mystery is remarkable.

Like asteroids, comets are leftovers from the formation of the solar system. They were probably created somewhere between the orbits of Saturn and Uranus. Many comets were pulled into the solar system by the *gravity* of these forming planets, but many others were flung nearly outside the solar system. Astronomers think that these distant travelers still orbit the Sun, 20,000 to 100,000 times farther away than the Earth. As many as 2 trillion ice balls may be slowly creeping around the Sun in space, where the temperatures are low enough to preserve them for billions of years. Occasionally, the gravity of a nearby star flings some of these ice balls back into the inner solar system, where we can watch their performances as comets.

You can see the long, wispy tail of the comet Kohoutek while it's making its close passage around the Sun. The tail travels away from the Sun because a solar wind pushes away the thin gas released by the melting comet nucleus.

Because comets make sudden appearances in the sky, ancient people believed that they were bringers of evil things or warnings of bad news. In some ways, they may have been correct. On rare occasions, comets have collided with Earth, causing great calamities.

One collision took place in Siberia in 1908. A comet nucleus slammed into the atmosphere and exploded several miles above a Siberian forest. Trees were flattened for many miles around. Fortunately, the site was not very populated. If the comet had hit a large city, however, much of the city would have been destroyed.

Comet collisions aren't always destructive. Some scientists believe that the ancient comets that collided with Earth may have delivered important chemicals, which made it possible for life to form here.

Falling Stars

Many ancient people also believed that stars could fall. If you watch the night sky for about an hour on any clear night, you should be able to spot between 3 and 15 "falling stars" streaking across the sky.

On November 12, 1833, observers watched meteors "falling from the sky like snowflakes." After reading about the meteor shower, an artist of the time created his version of the scene. These falling stars are actually very tiny bits of disintegrated comets entering Earth's atmosphere.

Falling stars are really *meteors*—tiny bits of space debris that are pulled by Earth's gravity into its atmosphere. Usually no bigger than grains of sand, these meteors shoot into Earth's atmosphere at speeds of 22,000 to 67,000 miles (35,400 to 107,800 kilometers) per hour—or at the rate of 6 to 18 miles (10 to 30 kilometers) per second. The air ahead of the speeding meteor is squeezed and heated so tremendously that it glows brightly. For a second or two, your eye sees a brilliant white streak against the black sky. Then the meteor is consumed by the intense heat and is gone.

Occasionally, if a meteor is large enough, it can survive the entire burning trip through the atmosphere and fall to Earth, blasting a crater into the ground. When meteors reach Earth's atmosphere, or the atmosphere of the Moon or other planets, they are called *meteorites*.

One especially famous meteorite fell in 1954. It smashed through the roof of a house in Alabama and grazed the leg of a woman sleeping inside. Fortunately, being hit by a meteorite is a rare event. This woman, who was left with only a very bad bruise, is the only person known to have been hit by a meteorite.

Another famous meteorite fell at least 25,000 years ago in the Arizona desert. This meteorite was as big as a house. It blasted a hole about ¾ mile (1.2 kilometers) in diameter and more than 600 feet (200 meters) deep.

Other large meteorites have formed craters on other places on Earth, but the process of *erosion* has smoothed so many that it is hard to tell exactly where the craters are. So scientists have learned to look below the land surface for rings of circular cracks that were made by the impacts of meteorites.

Finding craters on the Moon is a different story. Because the Moon does not have an atmosphere, marks on its surface last billions of years. The Moon is covered with millions of small and large meteorite craters.

About 25,000 years ago, a house-sized iron meteorite slammed into the Arizona desert, blasting a crater nearly 2,000 feet (600 meters) deep and about ¾ mile (1.2 kilometers) across.

Scientists sawed off this fragment of an iron meteorite to study it. By treating the surface with acids, they were able to see its interlocking crystal structure.

Astronomers are fascinated by meteorites because, except for the Moon rocks brought back to Earth by astronauts, they are the only pieces of the solar system we can study up close. Scientists estimate that, every year, more than 10,000 tons of meteors and meteorites fall to Earth. Most of that material simply burns up or falls into Earth's oceans.

Where They Come From

One of the important questions about meteors and meteorites is where do they come from? Scientists who study meteorites have found that they are made of iron and nickel metal, a mixture of iron and stone, or entirely of stone. Most appear to be fragments of large asteroids that collided with each other and were smashed apart.

These fragments, drifting randomly around the Sun, eventually collide with planets and moons.

Scientists believe that some meteorites are actually pieces of the Moon and Mars. When asteroids or big meteorites collided with the Moon and Mars, rocks were blasted off their surfaces and eventually fell to Earth.

Meteorites are pieces of asteroids, moons, or planets, but meteors are pieces of comets.

We know that comets contain dust. We also know that each time a comet gets near the Sun, its surface begins to melt, which releases the frozen dust in its nucleus. The dust particles spill out along the comet's orbit. While they are still in orbit, these dust particles are called *meteoroids*. When Earth passes through a comet's orbit, many of these dust particles fall into Earth's atmosphere

Some scientists believe this young meteorite—only 1,300 million years old—may have been knocked off Mars after the planet was struck by a huge meteorite. The fragment drifted through space for millions of years and eventually fell to Earth. Scientists found it in Antarctica.

Scientists believe that the Antarctica meteorite was formed from two different basalt rocks. The inside surface of the meteorite shows a few cracks and dark glossy areas. Scientists discovered that the gases in these dark spots matched the gases in the atmosphere of Mars, which were measured by the *Viking* landing spacecraft in 1976.

and glow brightly for a moment. When they enter Earth's atmosphere, they are called meteors.

Sometimes, as many as 60 meteors fall in an hour. This is called a *meteor shower*. When Earth does not pass through a comet's orbit, stray meteors from ancient comets that have long since disappeared still fall in its atmosphere, but at a much slower rate.

The Mystery of the Squashed Comet

How did the comet P/Shoemaker-Levy 9 break apart? Astronomers found the answer by tracing the comet's orbit. They calculated that on July 8, 1992, the parent comet, an object about 6 miles (9 kilometers) in diameter, passed only 15,500 miles (25,000 kilometers) above the cloud tops of Jupiter. Jupiter's strong gravity created stress in the comet, which tore it apart.

That wasn't the first time a comet had broken apart this way. During the last two centuries, astronomers have observed at least 25 comets that have broken up. What makes the Shoemaker comet special, however, is what happened to the fragments.

Over the course of the next year, the scientists thought, the 21 fragments would travel far out from Jupiter, turn, and come falling back. From July 16 through July 22, 1994, all of the fragments would crash into the giant planet.

This astronomical event of the century had one hitch. When the fragments hit, they would be just around the far side of Jupiter and not directly visible through Earth-based telescopes. Although the actual moments of impact would not be visible, the sites of the impacts would quickly come into view because of the fast rotation of the planet.

Scientists combined a photo of Jupiter with a photo of comet P/Shoemaker-Levy 9 so that they could see how fragments of the comet fell toward the planet.

When the week arrived, astronomers around the world were ready. The fragments began slamming into the planet one at a time, at speeds of 37 miles (60 kilometers) per second. Over several days, each fragment burrowed a deep hole in Jupiter's atmosphere and exploded. The total force of their impacts was equal to that of about 200 billion tons of dynamite exploding at once!

When Jupiter rotated so that the impact sites came into view, astronomers were dazzled. Pictures taken by the Hubble Space Telescope and other observatories re-

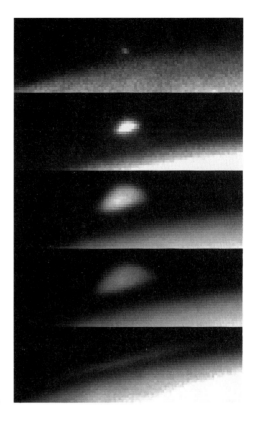

The blast of one fragment of the comet P/Shoemaker-Levy 9 was seen in the atmosphere just beyond Jupiter's edge. It took a little more than 10 minutes for the large fireball (top) to spread into a broad, flat cloud.

vealed new Earth-sized dark spots in Jupiter's upper atmosphere. One spot even had a dark ring around it, giving the site the appearance of a black eye. In a short time, winds circling the planet spread the spots until they joined and formed a small band around the planet.

For years to come, astronomers will study the data they collected during the impact of the comet P/Shoemaker-Levy 9 on Jupiter. They will try to learn about the composition of the comet and of Jupiter itself. The explosions stirred up Jupiter's atmosphere and brought up gases that normally remain well below Jupiter's cloud tops. Astronomers will learn about the wind forces in Jupiter's atmosphere by watching the changes in the shapes of the dark spots over time. Other scientists, using instruments that measure things we cannot see, such as radio waves and X rays, will use their data to learn more about Jupiter, too.

The impact of the comet P/Shoemaker-Levy 9 on Jupiter has given astronomers a better understanding of

As Jupiter rotated on its axis, NASA's Hubble Space Telescope was able to photograph one of the sites where the comet struck the planet's surface. The point of impact looked something like a "black eye."

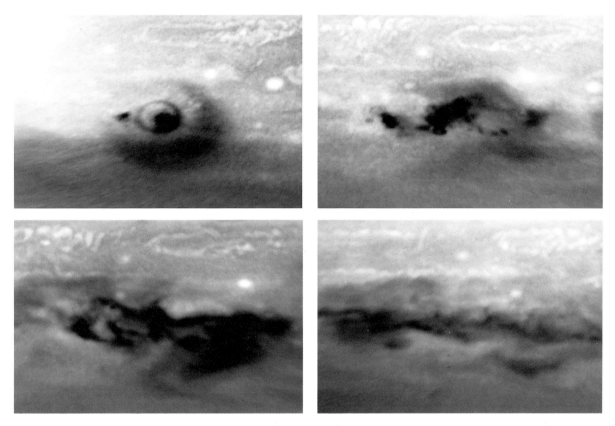

Over a period of a few weeks, the marks left by the comet began to disperse in Jupiter's winds and spread out around the surface of the planet.

the smaller objects that orbit our Sun. It also causes them to wonder what would happen if an object as large as that comet struck Earth? Comets, asteroids, and meteorites have collided with Earth in the past. In fact, some scientists believe that 65 million years ago a big asteroid might have collided with Earth and caused dinosaurs to become extinct.

Sixty-five million years ago, an asteroid or comet slammed into Earth along the coastline of Mexico's Yucatan peninsula. The resulting shock waves, dust, and heat affected the entire Earth. Many scientists now believe that the impact caused the extinction of dinosaurs and about 70 percent of all life forms on the planet.

Fortunately, collisions of big objects are extremely rare. But what if another one is on its way? Is there anything we could do about it? Many scientists wonder about that, too.

QUICK FACTS

The values in these charts are approximate. As astronomers continue to gather new data, they refine their calculations.

LARGE ASTEROIDS

Name	Diameter		Distance from Sun*
	(Miles)	(Kilometers)	
1 Ceres	578	930	2.8
2 Pallas	343	552	2.8
4 Vesta	324	521	2.4
10 Hygeia	260	419	3.1
704 Interamnia	203	327	3.1
511 Davida	200	322	3.2
52 Europa	183	295	3.1
87 Sylvia	171	277	3.5
65 Cybele	167	269	3.4
15 Eunomia	161	259	2.6

SEVERAL COMETS

Name	Orbital Period	Close Point from Sun*	Far Point from Sun*
	(years)		
Halley	76.09	0.6	35.3
Encke	3.3	0.34	4.1
Bennett	1,680	0.54	281.9
Kohoutek	75,000**	0.14	?
West	500,000**	0.2	?

* Times the distance from Earth to Sun, 93 million miles (149.6 million kilometers)
** Rough estimate
? Unknown or Very Approximate

METEOR SHOWERS

Shower Name	Approximate Dates	Hourly Rate	Associated Comet
Quadrantids	January 2–4	30	
Lyrids	April 20–24	8	1861 I
Eta Aquarids	May 2–7	10	Halley (?)
Delta Aquarids	July 26–31	15	
Perseids	August 10–14	40	1982 III
Orionids	October 18–23	15	Halley (?)
Taurids	November 2–4	8	Encke
Leonids	November 14–19	6	1866 I Tempel
Geminids	December 10–13	50	

GLOSSARY

Asteroid
Small rock or metal body orbiting the Sun, primarily between the orbits of Mars and Jupiter.

Asteroid Belt
A ring of asteroids orbiting the Sun between Mars and Jupiter.

Astronomer
A scientist who studies objects in space.

Coma
The glowing head of a comet that forms when the comet is near the Sun and gas is released.

Comet
A small icy body that orbits the Sun and produces a tail of gas and dust when it is warmed by the Sun's heat.

Diameter
The width of a round or sphere-shaped object.

Erosion	Forces in nature, such as glaciers and running water, that wear away the land and carry away debris.
Gravity	A force that causes objects to attract each other.
Inner Asteroid Belt	A band of widely spaced asteroids that orbit the Sun at a distance of less than 250 million miles (400 million kilometers).
Meteor	A particle of comet dust that burns up and glows when it enters Earth's atmosphere.
Meteorite	A piece of space rock or metal that collides with the surface of a planet or moon.
Meteoroid	A meteor, before it enters Earth's atmosphere.
Meteor Shower	An event in which many meteors, following the same orbit or parallel orbits, enter Earth's atmosphere at the same time.
Nucleus	The solid, icy part of a comet.
Orbit	The path of an asteroid, comet, meteor, planet, or other satellite when traveling around the Sun.
Outer Asteroid Belt	A band of widely spaced asteroids that orbit the Sun at a distance of more than 250 million miles (400 million kilometers).
Solar System	The sun and its orbiting planets and moons.
Solar Wind	Electrically charged particles that are thrown outward from the Sun.

FOR FURTHER READING

Asimov, Isaac. *Comets and Meteors.* Milwaukee, Wisconsin: Gareth Stevens, 1989.

Brewer, Duncan. *Comets, Asteroids and Meteorites.* New York: Marshall Cavendish, 1992.

Gallant, Ray A. *Our Universe.* Washington, D.C.: National Geographic Society, 1986.

Lauber, Patricia. *Voyagers From Space: Meteors and Meteorites.* New York: Crowell, 1989.

Miller, Ron, and Hartmann, William K. *The Grand Tour, A Traveler's Guide to the Solar System.* Rev. ed. New York: Workman Publishing, 1993.

Vogt, Gregory L. *The Search for the Killer Asteroid.* Brookfield, Connecticut: The Millbrook Press, 1994.

————. *Halley's Comet: What We've Learned.* New York: Franklin Watts, 1987.

INDEX

ABOUT THE AUTHOR

Gregory L. Vogt works for NASA's Education Division at the Johnson Space Center in Houston, Texas. He works with astronauts in developing educational videos for schools.

Mr. Vogt previously served as the executive director of the Discovery World Museum of Science, Economics and Technology in Milwaukee, Wisconsin, and as an eighth-grade science teacher. He holds bachelor's and master's degrees in science from the University of Wisconsin at Milwaukee, as well as a doctorate in curriculum and instruction from Oklahoma State University.